# PET OWNER'S GUIDE TO THE
# RHODESIAN RIDGEBACK

## Stig G. Carlson

RINGPRESS

# ABOUT THE AUTHOR

Stig G. Carlson, a Swedish national born in Finland, started his life in dogs in 1968, and he now has an international reputation as a breeder, author and lecturer specialising in Rhodesian Ridgebacks. His seminars have a wide following and he has travelled as far afield as South Africa, the USA, England, Israel and Australia on judging and lecturing appointments.

Stig has acted as Chairman of the Swedish Ridgeback Club, Chairman of the Stockholm Kennel Club, Vice Chair and Chairman of the SSD (parent club of some 80 breeds) in Sweden, and participated in the Swedish Kennel Club's 100th year anniversary team. In 1988 he chaired the second Ridgeback World Congress, and in 1997 he received the Swedish Kennel Club Merits Award.

## PHOTOGRAPHY

STIG G. CARLSON

Published by Ringpress Books,
Vincent Lane, Dorking, Surrey,
RH4 3YX, England.

First published 1998
© Interpet Publishing. All rights reserved

**ISBN 1 86054 058 9**

Printed in Hong Kong through Printworks Int. Ltd.

# CONTENTS

## TRAINING YOUR RIDGEBACK 40

**4** Typical behaviour; Guarding; Words of wisdom; Fighting; On your bike; Basic commands; Sports; Agility; Coursing; Dog shows; Preparing for the show.

## BREEDING RIDGEBACKS 55

**5** Should you breed?; Genetics; Genetics of ridges; Arrival of the puppies.

## HEALTH ISSUES 68

**6** Puppy nutrition; Feeding the adult; First aid; Vaccinations; Hereditary faults; Lack of ridge; Dermoid sinus; Dermoid cyst; Kinked tails; Hip dysplasia; Parvovirus; Rabies; Caring for the veteran.

# 1 Origins And Development

The Rhodesian Ridgeback is the only officially recognised dog that originates from Southern Africa, and is one of the few breeds of which we know more about its character and functional ability than we do of its measurable size and shape. It is also the only breed which gives owners of these dogs a chance to live with a piece of recent history – the era of lion hunting, of the

*Lion hunting gave the breed its fame, and its first name – the Lion Dog.*

final colonisation of Southern Africa, and of the last great adventurers, who became legends in their own lifetime. Living with and understanding the Rhodesian Ridgeback also requires something special of the owner, for it is a demanding dog and should not be taken on lightly.

This book is for everyone whose heart yearns for that little bit extra, that little piece of the wild nature that is in, and must remain in, every Ridgeback.

In the beginning, the Ridgeback was not a single breed of dog at all, but a group of dogs performing specific functions.

Destiny had, however, given a distinctive characteristic to a number of individual dogs, irrespective of their shape, colour, size or long-forgotten name. Some of these dogs possessed a hair formation in the shape of a ridge along the back; a unique natural feature which made them the focus of attention.

At about the same time as these ridged dogs were attracting attention, in the latter part of the 19th century, the world was becoming increasingly globalized, and spectacular sports and hobbies became the 'in thing' for the rich, the daring, and also for the famous. Foremost among these pastimes was big game hunting, and shooting a lion in Africa, or a tiger in India, was considered the ultimate test of bravery and skill. Against the backdrop of these last fading years of colonial expansion, the Ridgeback was born as a breed. Lion hunting gave the breed its fame, and its first name, The Lion Dog.

As early as 1923, a year after the very first organised meeting was held to discuss the breed (which was, as yet, not even established as a breed), a British vet was writing in Farmers Weekly: "The number of lions is rapidly decreasing in Rhodesia, and with them also the number of lion hunters. It would be a real pity if this great breed of dog (the lion dog) should become extinct. There are still many uses well suited for this dog, even if one has to consider it unlikely that it will ever become a large dog breed."

Dogs have existed in Africa since prehistoric times. These cave paintings are in Zimbabwe.

*Boer dog as shown in the Vortrekker monument in Pretoria. This typical mixed breed does not indicate a ridge, but this is what many Boer companions must have looked like.*

## THE LEGEND

Legends are, in many cases, romantic descriptions of the truth. In others they are beautiful fairytales, but they are not without importance, as legends have a tendency to create positive interest and focus attention on their subject.

If you were to believe the more far-fetched theories about the origin of the ridge – the unusual hair formation on the back of the dogs, which is today refined into an elegant ridge with two crowns under a symmetrical arch – the Phoenicians brought dogs with these formations to Africa from the East. It is a fact that there are ridged dogs on the island of Phu Quoc, in the Gulf of Thailand, also in Thailand and, presumably, in Cambodia. Another theory is that traders, be they Phoenicians, Arabs, Portuguese, or Dutch, took the original, semi-wild African dogs, some of which had the genes for a ridged hair formation on their backs, from Africa to the Far East.

*Today's Ridgeback is forever linked to the colonisation of Southern Africa.*

There is one point to keep in mind when speculating about these legends, and that is that it does not matter where the dogs originated. Today's ridged dogs in Thailand are Spitz-type dogs, and it is a mistake to call them 'Thai Ridgebacks'. They are exciting dogs, but they should correctly be referred to as Thai Ridged Dogs, or Thai Ridged Spitzes.

The Ridgeback, as we know it, is a breed that has developed in Africa over the last 300 years, for use as a hunting and guard dog. It has inherited the hair formation on its back from a number of dogs with that quality, who lived in Southern Africa during that period. There is a story that Egyptian dogs, of Slughi type, have shown ridgelike formations along their backs and, in that grand old bible of dogs, *Hutchinson's Dog Encyclopedia,* there is, on page 836, a picture of three Sloughis from the last years of the 19th century, one of which clearly has a ridge. Of course, this may confirm the legend about the ancient North African heritage of the ridged dogs, but it could equally – and this is more likely – prove that love knows no boundaries, not even breed boundaries.

It is likely that Portuguese traders, who captured some Hottentots in the late 15th century, left the earliest written evidence of what was to become the ridge. They described the faithful dogs kept by the Hottentots as "ugly and hyena-like, with a funny hair bending forwards on their backs." But they also noted that these creatures seemed devoted to, and trusted by, their masters.

The history of Africa, like the history of most of our world, is the history of conquerors and the conquered, of movement and change. The Hottentots drove the bushmen further and further south, the Bantus drove the Hottentots out, the great Zulu warriors captured vast areas of south-east Africa, all of which caused turbulence, both in population distribution and lifestyles. I have seen small, Basenji/hyena type semi-domesticated dogs in the wilder parts of Zimbabwe and I have some carvings from the interior of Benin, showing Spitz-type dogs with markings on their backs.

In the annals of Dr Livingstone's famous journeys through the interior of Africa we have illustrations showing small, almost Cape Hunting Dog-type creatures, with bushlike hair formations on their backs. The author Laurens van der Post, has added to the charming Ridgeback legends by including the breed in some of his stories. This all helps to prove that ridged dogs have existed in Africa for centuries, until they have become part of African legend, as well as of the continent's history.

The legends about ancient African tribes and their dogs do have a scientific background insofar as it has been proved beyond doubt that the old indigenous types of dog did carry the ridged hair formation. Mylda Arsenis, in her book Ridged Dogs in Africa, refers to the Austrian Professor von Schulmuth, whose diggings in 1936 unearthed the remains of Hottentot dogs that had been buried by river mud centuries earlier. The best preserved of the specimens showed a clear 'ridge' on its back.

The dog was reported to have had a broad, flat skull, and pricked ears.

The Zulus were very impressed by 'the dogs with a snake mark on their backs' because of the exceptional courage these dogs showed, but it is unclear if the Zulus themselves took these indigenous dogs into their households.

Early legends about ridged dogs must also include those of the Boers and their house dogs, named after the distinctive hair formations they must frequently have shown: Verkeerdehaar (literally, false hair), Maanhaar (moon hair), Vuilbaard (soiled beard) and the legendary guard dog, the Steekbard (spiky beard). If the paintings, drawings or carpets depicting the Great Trek (the Boer migration away from English oppression which began in 1835, culminating in the battle of Blood River in 1838 between the Boers and the Zulus, and finally ending in 1854) could speak, what tales would they tell of canine bravery and devotion!

An old Rhodesian source summarises the early days of the ridged dogs well: "The Lion Dog is a valuable hunting dog of unknown origin. The breed shows very strong mental capability." Those characteristics, not least the intelligence combined with bravery, also created a legend among the African population that the ridged dogs had a drop of lion blood in their veins.

The legendary lion hunt became the call to fame for the Ridgeback. The ridged dogs never attacked, or attempted to kill, the lion, but used their exceptional mobility, their stamina, and their power to move fast enough to avoid the claws of the lion, while keeping it at bay until the hunter arrived.

In more recent times, the Ridgeback has been used to hunt down and kill wild boars in Africa, New Zealand, Australia and in the state of Tennessee, USA. There are also recorded instances of Ridgebacks killing cheetahs and baboons. Using the skills learned in lion hunting, the Ridgeback has succeeded well when hunting cougar in Canada, the USA and Mexico.

While the Ridgeback is famous for its reputation as the old 'Lion Dog', we must not forget the other basic qualities of the breed, which are those of a trustworthy guard dog and of a reliable family pet, famous for its patience with children.

*As hunters, the ridged dogs showed intelligence, agility and courage.*

## THE FACTS

There are two specific periods which were important to the development of the modern Rhodesian Ridgeback, which were when the breed originated and when it was formalised. In 1652 the Dutch, under Jan van Riebeeck, established a small garrison in the Cape. The first organised establishment brought fewer than 100 people, but they brought enough livestock to enable the garrison to become self-sufficient as soon as possible. This was essential in order to keep down costs and make the colony financially viable. This was not the first encounter, by any means, between Europeans and the natives, who were mainly Hottentots. Portuguese and Dutch adventurers had landed at the Cape before this and, when a Dutch ship was stranded there five years before Riebeeck's landing, they even found a Hottentot who spoke some English! However, with the establishment of the first Dutch garrison, a systematic inflow of people and farm implements, livestock, and also domestic animals began. We know for sure there were dogs, but we can only speculate on their breeds. We do know that the Dutch had an official policy of 'learning to use all indigenous resources as much as possible', so serious attempts were made to communicate with the local population, and to understand the local natural history. As the colony became established, other Europeans arrived to swell the population, notably French Huguenots, who began to arrive from 1688.

By 1707, when there were 803 adults and 820 children in the Cape area, the colonisation of the interior began. Europeans continued to emigrate to Southern Africa, and throughout the 18th century they developed a distinctive way of life suited to the climate and the country. Following a British naval victory

*Ridged dogs served as guard dogs on African farms on a large scale.*

in 1795, which ended the Dutch East India Company's rule in the Cape, the first British Governor arrived in 1807. It was during these early centuries in the history of South Africa that the first deliberate matings between European dogs and African ridged dogs must have taken place.

The second, and decisive, period in the development of the breed was in the years between 1870 and 1922. During these years the unique hunting and guarding capabilities of certain types of dogs were recognised until, in 1922, some enthusiasts got together to write down guidelines for what they hoped would become an independent breed. In the 1870s, Reverend Charles Helm travelled to the south of modern-day Zimbabwe, in those days named Rhodesia, accompanied by two ridged dogs which he had acquired in Swellendam in the Cape district. The well-known big game hunter, Cornelius van Rooyen, tried these dogs when out hunting and found them excellent for the purpose. He then mated these dogs with just about any other type of dog that showed the necessary hunting abilities. In his enthusiasm, van Rooyen recommended these

ridged dogs to other big game hunters, and gradually the comcious mating of able hunting dogs with ridged dogs of hunting type took place. The popularity of these exceptional animals grew so fast that they, for some time, were even called van Rooyen's dogs, and later, Lion Dogs.

There are notes of a discussion between van Rooyen's son and a Mr Welling, regarding the first dogs van Rooyen received, and about his breeding of them. The conversation suggests that the original dogs Rev Helm brought from the Cape were considerably larger than later ridged dogs "with enormous courage but little scenting power." Van Rooyen was said to have crossed the original dogs with lighter dogs to add speed, eg. Airedales, Collies and Pointers (the Pointer crosses were not considered to be much good). There are also reliable notes about other breeds having been crossed with the ridged dogs early in our century. The fact is the Ridgeback of today is a mixture. The vast size of Southern Africa, and the relatively slow pace of transport 60 to 90 years ago, means that the breeding of dogs was somewhat hit and miss. Hence, it is also realistic to assume that ridged

*The breed's popularity is now widespread. Photo: C. Goethberg.*

dogs in various parts of Southern, and soon also Eastern, Africa even had different genetic backgrounds. (Just look at the ears of some Ridgebacks today, and you see that old blood can appear and influence this part of the dog – and naturally his other qualities.)

It is likely that the most famous of all the hunters, Frederick Courtney Selous, got his ridged dogs directly from van Rooyen. Selous, whom Kaiser Wilhelm I called "a good example to his country's youth" and President Roosevelt considered 'his personal friend', was to become the model for Alan Quartermain in Rider Haggard's book *King Solomon's Mines*, and also Sean Courtney in Wilbur Smith's African epic saga beginning with *When the Lion Feeds*.

A number of well-known hunters followed in the footsteps of van Rooyen and Selous, such as H.A. Fraser, Mrs Foljambe, Mr Upcher and the Kenyan, Sydney Waller. This tradition continued right into the 1960s when, by 1966, Lewis Christian was said to have shot 226 lions. He was always accompanied by at least two Ridgebacks.

In order to gain an understanding of the breed, it is

important to take note of some of the comments made by these early pioneers. R.H. Fraser wrote in 1932, in material later published by his daughter, about his Ridgeback bitch Jess: "She was fast, and clever, and brave. She was paralysed by a fall, but recovered. She was taken from the veranda by a leopard, but escaped, clawed by a lion, blinded by a spitting cobra, and recovered."

Fraser also noted: "The old Afrikaner hunters, van Rooyen and others, who adventured north of the Limpopo, evolved the Ridgeback breed because they required a dog which was bold enough to bay up dangerous game, such as lion and leopard, yet too clever to rush in and get killed."

In 1922 Francis Richard Barnes, who had owned ridged dogs for quite a number of years, called a meeting to discuss formalising the ridged dogs as a breed. Barnes used the old Dalmatian Standard as a basis, for logistical purposes. Not a bad choice – and a symbolic move. The ridged dogs of the 1920s were hunting dogs, with good guarding qualities, akin to a number of traditional European hunting dogs. The very first Standard, or description, did give the same height for males and females, at a maximum 71 centimetres, a figure that has since been adjusted a number of times over the years. Some of the other points agreed in 1922 are the same as many quoted in today's official Ridgeback Standard, reflecting much of what Barnes and his colleagues described over 70 years ago.

Before moving into the last decade of the 20th century and looking at today's dogs, two facts must be borne in mind that have a direct bearing on how we interpret the Ridgebacks these days.

Firstly, the two basic uses of ridged dogs were developed in parallel, and equally appreciated. As hunters, the ridged dogs showed intelligence, agility, and courage, and a unique ability to survive in the face of danger. As guard dogs they not only kept away unwanted human visitors from the farms, but they also showed a remarkable skill in keeping the place clear of raiding baboons. Reading the old stories by hunters and game wardens, one can also appreciate what distances the early Ridgebacks had to travel as they followed their masters, who had the benefit of a horse to ride.

Secondly, the ridged dogs, which came to be referred to as Ridgebacks after the 1920s, were already more widespread in those days than one tends to think. In the 1930s the breed existed as a guard dog on the tobacco plantations, which were the main farming business in Rhodesia and Nyasaland (present-day Malawi), and was kept by other farmers all over Southern Africa, in Mozambique and also in Kenya. While the spectacular hunting abilities, and the equally colourful lives of Selous, van Rooyen and Fraser, gave the breed visibility, numerically, the Ridgeback is likely to have served more as a guard dog than as a hunting dog. This is another quality in the dog that we can still appreciate to the full today. For instance, during the 75th anniversary celebrations in Harare in 1997, a group of solid, sturdy 'farm dogs' was paraded. They were hardly hunters, but they were examples of what the true guardians must have looked like last century.

In modern times, a number of famous people have owned Ridgebacks. The present Queen of England, when still Princess Elizabeth, was given two Ridgebacks, from which early UK champions are said to have descended. The actor Errol Flynn had Ridgebacks, and so did the former prime minister of Rhodesia, Ian Smith, who is still the patron of the parent club in Harare. He told me recently that he will never in his life live without a few Ridgebacks. Some years ago Hollywood produced a movie featuring a Ridgeback. All this, in combination with the fact that Ridgebacks have grown fast both numerically, and in visibility, on several continents, has led to the breed's present status, where the Ridgeback is no longer a minor breed. In dog show circles, this has become a breed that has, though not yet often, gone on to win Best in Show at major international all-breed dog shows.

As a result of this a much greater responsibility falls on Ridgeback owners to face up to the reality of the type of dog they have fallen in love with.

# 2 Breed Characteristics

Every breed has its own Standard, which is a written description of the 'perfect' dog. Obviously, there is no such thing as a completely faultless specimen, but the judge in the show ring assesses all entrants against the Standard, to evaluate how closely they conform to the blueprint. The winning dogs are those who are likely to produce future generations that possess true breed type, showing the physical and temperamental attributes that make the Rhodesian Ridgeback unique.

## EVALUATING THE BREED

Below, you will find my personal understanding of what the Ridgeback should be like. Having spent a long life closely related to the world of sports, my guiding star is *functionability*.

## THE ENTITY

A Ridgeback is a proud, elegant dog, whose body has a rectangular, but never quadratic, appearance. It is a classic hunting dog, so look for body proportions with a ratio of 5:4, length to height. It can be slightly, but not much, more than this. A body with these proportions produces the most effective gait for a dog that was required to cover long, tiring distances, before a possible hunt even began. The overall word to describe a good Ridgeback is balance. He should be strong, but not too heavy; powerful, but never clumsy; elegant, but never weak, or sleek like a greyhound; fast, but not the fastest; agile as few other dog breeds can be; and with staying power and energy. My motto is: There is only one extreme feature in a Ridgeback, and that is the total absence of extremes.

## THE HEAD

The Ridgeback head is that of a traditional hunter, with equal proportions between width and length of skull, as well as skull width or length to muzzle length.

*A correct Ridgeback head has even proportions between muzzle length, and length and width of skull.*

*A dark-nosed dog must have dark eyes. A liver-nosed dog would be expected to have amber eyes.*

*The muzzle and toplines must be parallel with a reasonably well-defined stop.*

*The correct male head has the same equal proportions, but shows a good degree of masculinity.*

Remember the proportions 1:1:1, and you have a good starting point. Added to this, the muzzle should be strong, with a correct set of teeth, and a good stop. The skull topline and that of the muzzle must be parallel. The Ridgeback head should never give a triangular impression, either seen from the side, or viewed from the front. Bitches should show clearly feminine features, and males have a strong masculine look to them.

## THE BODY
Any hunter, or runner, needs a strong base for long, hopefully well-trained, muscles. The sound

*The Ridgeback should present a balanced picture of power, strength and agility.*

Ridgeback must have a long neck, that is not too thick and heavy, and a well-shaped front. The pro-sternum or breastbone must be clearly visible from the side. The legs should have strong muscles, with sufficient, yet never heavy or round, bones. The shoulder should be sloping, forming an angle of approximately 30 degrees with an imaginary line drawn vertically through the top part of the shoulder bone (the scapula), to the ground.

The chest is deep to accommodate large lungs and, in an adult Ridgeback, should reach down to the elbows. But the chest and front should never be too broad, as this would hamper the swift, unpredictable zig-zag turns which the true Ridgeback exhibits when in hunting mode.

The ribcage should be of sufficient length, and end in an elegant curve towards the rear. A short ribcage combined with a long loin gives a weak topline and less endurance.

## THE RIDGE

The ridge is a symmetrical formation of hair growing in the opposite direction on the back of

*The ideal ridge starts directly behind the shoulder blades and extends to a point in line with the hip bones.*

point of the ridge. The arch must never be longer than one third of the total length of the ridge, including the arch. The ideal width of the ridge below the arch is 3–6 cms, depending on the size of the dog. The ridge is tapered towards the end.

## THE FEET AND LEGS

The feet should be rather high, with strong, well-arched toes, giving the dog the ability to climb. Short toes are a fault, as is a flat foot, which leads to less stamina in motion.

If you have not seen a Ridgeback in motion you have not seen a Ridgeback. It is essential that the angles of the front and hind feet are equal, giving the feet equal 'stretch', or ground coverage.

the dog. The ideal ridge starts directly behind the shoulder blades and extends to a point in line with the hip bones. At the front end the ridge has two whorls, called crowns, symmetrically placed on each side of the ridge. Any other formation, either in the number or position, is considered incorrect. Above the crowns there is an arch, a symmetrical, bowed, or arch-shaped formation at the starting

## THE TAIL

Attention should be paid to the root of the tail, i.e. the thick, first 10–15 cms of the tail. It is this part of the tail that is the decisive indicator, never mind about the rest of it. The root of the tail should be parallel with the ground in slow movement, if the croup is well balanced. Both a high-set root to the tail, and a rounded, sloping croup with a low-set tail,

*The Ridgeback should appear clean-cut and muscular, with sound front and hind angulation.*

the dog's hind legs reach too far forward under the front feet, forcing the dog to 'crab', that is, to move sideways in order to avoid a collision between front and rear feet. He also covers too short a distance behind.

It is important that the front feet do not point excessively outwards when standing still, and that the front, seen facing the dog, is not too broad. The English term 'barrel chest' is a good warning signal for an unwanted width and heaviness of the chest.

## PACES

The well-balanced Ridgeback, or any dog with similar conformation, covers an equal amount of ground in trot – with ground contact – in front as in the rear.

A sound, effective trot is also only possible in a dog with a correctly proportioned body, i.e. where the body is more long than high. This is where the 5:4 proportions between length and height become relevant.

The front feet should move with low, effective strides, almost caressing the ground. High front feet movements, the famous 'hackney gait', similar to that exhibited by hackney horses,

signal weaknesses in the croup.

It is important to evaluate the quality of the croup in a Ridgeback. The root of the tail is a good indicator, as, with a steep croup, the root of the tail points upward of the imaginary extension of the topline of the dog when he is in fast trot. If the croup is too sloping, the root of the tail points downward.

In the case of a high tail-root and a steep croup, the dog might kick far behind when trotting, but he does not cover sufficient ground under the body and normally leaves the last decimetres of the 'long hind stride' to become a kick in the air. With a sloping croup, indicate a straight front, which severely hampers the movements of the dog.

A Ridgeback can move quite fast, and this, combined with his ability to make agile sideways movements, makes him one of the fastest breeds in the world when competing in canine sports such as Lure Coursing.

## AGILITY

A well-built Ridgeback can turn and twist at very high speed, which was a major factor in the breed's success when hunting big game.

The ability to turn and twist has sometimes, incorrectly, been attributed to a short and compact body, but in the Ridgeback it is the muscular, rather flexible, connection between the ribcage and the shoulders and front legs which is the main source of flexibility. This is why the ribcage should be deep, but not be too broad, and never round as in a 'barrel chest'. The Ridgeback, in full gallop, moves his hind legs outside the front legs, almost as a greyhound does, making full use of his hardworking, flexible back.

## TEMPERAMENT

The founding father of the Breed Standard, F.R. Barnes, wrote: "... one would expect just such characteristics as the Ridgeback so markedly shows: speed, power, courage, fidelity and affection, and in addition a remarkable skill in tackling wild animals."

The courage goes with the hunting ability. Let us, though, correct a possible

*The Ridgeback can turn and twist at high speed. This is one of the features that makes him a big game hunter*

misinterpretation of courage. The Ridgeback is notably 'smart', with an inbuilt survival instinct. This is not a dog that throws itself head first into danger, but one with the natural instinct to avoid it. Many a so-called canine intelligence test goes badly wrong when it tries to measure the 'courage level' of a Ridgeback by, for instance, expecting him to attack a padded arm on command. A little incident that occurred in a large park in New York says it all: An owner was walking his Collie and his Ridgeback late one evening, when a man, at least six feet tall, approached. The attacker kicked the Collie, which disappeared, crying. Despite warnings from the dog owner, the attacker then directed a kick at the Ridgeback. But there was no dog there to kick. In a second the Ridgeback appeared from the other side, and pinned the attacker to a tree. The assailant was not seriously damaged, at least not physically, but he was kept standing very still until the law arrived.

The Ridgeback is even-tempered, but can be somewhat aloof towards strangers. He has great patience with children, but, if not treated with respect, will let his tormentor know. However, he seldom inflicts anything more than a gentle warning.

*Even-tempered and companionable with his own family, the Ridgeback can be aloof with strangers.* Photo: H. Loefkvist.

The other main quality of the Ridgeback is that of a good guard dog, and with this comes self-confidence. In the show ring the Ridgeback is expected to be curious, on his own terms, without being overly enthusiastic towards judges or other officials. An adult Ridgeback is very seldom, and should never be, aggressive towards human beings. He can though, if not well trained, create havoc at shows simply by misbehaving. Here the fault is with the owner, not the dog. On the other hand, if an adult Ridgeback shows clear signs of insecurity or fear, beware, for this is a sign of faulty temperament, or of a dog that has been badly treated. I would not fear a Ridgeback who is merely misbehaving, for he would only be following his instincts, but I do have many, and clear, reservations about approaching a dog as strong as the Ridgeback if he signals insecurity or fear.

A typical feature of the Ridgeback temperament is that he has a very, very long memory. Treat a Ridgeback well, and he will remember it for the rest of his life. Treat him badly and ...well, the same rule applies, but to your disadvantage.

## FAULTS

Naturally there are disqualifying faults in a Ridgeback. Too light a coat colour, without warmth to it, or too dark a colour. A dark mahogany shade without the red nuances, silver, and brindle, are all incorrect colours. An excessive amount of white colouring, particularly on the belly or inner sides of the legs, is also a disqualifying fault, as is excessive solid black pigmentation other than on the muzzle and ear tips. The lack of a ridge, or more, or less, than two crowns, or clearly asymmetrical crowns, self evidently disqualify the dog in the show ring.

## THE TRUE TYPE

The Ridgeback is one of the very few, if not the only, breed in which functionality is type. The breed was standardised, not because of how the dogs looked, but based upon how how they performed. So, forget physical details, such as some small patches of white hair, or a centimetre too little, or too much, in height. Look at the entity. Breeders need to consider every aspect of the dog, such as keeping the size balanced over a long period of time, but each single Ridgeback must be judged

*Every Ridgeback must be judged on his own individual qualities. This bitch shows true Championship qualities.*

on his own individual qualities. Look for length in the body, which will make the dog a better mover. Equally, make sure his front and hind quarters are at the correct angle to each other, to allow the sweeping, almost catlike, movements. Check that the chest is strong and deep enough to provide a basis for endurance, and make sure the individual dog has the correct temperament. He should not be aggressive, but not necessarily over-friendly either, and must be self-assured, almost to the point of arrogance.

In addition to the physical features and the temperament, I want to add that part of a true Ridgeback type is that the individual is in good physical condition. The muscles should be well-developed and well-trained. Being a good long-distance runner, a Ridgeback should have rather long and elegant muscles, not the short, rounded muscles associated with a dog bred for sprinting over fairly short distances.

Having said all this, when you look at the true Ridgeback, you should be able to imagine that he would have done well among van Rooyen's hunters, or see him, in your mind's eye, at his home in the wide spaces of Africa, guarding his farm and family!

# 3 The Ridgeback Puppy

If you are not already a dog owner, there are five basic questions you will, or should, be asking yourself before you begin the process of becoming one.

- Shall I have a dog?
- What breed of dog am I attracted to and will it suit my lifestyle – in this case, why choose a Ridgeback?
- What are my plans, dreams, and ambitions for the puppy? If the answer is 'playmate only' today, am I sure I will not want to consider breeding from my dog later on?
- What makes a Ridgeback puppy different?
- The first 10 months – what must I remember to do?

The question of having a dog must always be considered as a long-term commitment, and it must be a decision in which the entire family is involved. I take it for granted that the honoured reader would never consider buying a puppy as a Christmas gift to a child.

Examine your lifestyle, and consider how you live?

Is your home near to a park, or do you have access to open space, or live in the country? How big a flat or house do you have? Do you have young children? And, most importantly, is there anyone at home to take care of the puppy when he is young? If the answer to the last question is "No", do not even consider buying a dog. A puppy, or adolescent dog, cannot, and should not, be left alone for long periods of time while you are out at work.

When you are considering whether to have a dog, do realise that all of us have stressful periods in our lives. Are you prepared to remain calm and friendly towards

*Puppies are irresistible, but it is important to remember that the Ridgeback will develop into a large and demanding adult.*
*Photo: H. Splengler.*

your dog, when everything is going wrong at work or at home? Your dog cannot be allowed to suffer just because we human beings live a stressful life. However, if you know you can maintain the right attitude, I can guarantee that caring about a dog who is truly a trustworthy companion is one of the best ways of relaxing, and of feeling your true worth.

## MATCHING LIFESTYLES

Assuming that you are already attracted to the Ridgeback, there are a few points to note.

First of all, consider what the dog will look like when it is older, not how it looks as a puppy.

Some breeds are much more suited to city life, with less need for long periods of physical exercise daily, but do not make the mistake of thinking that a Toy dog, whose mobility is far less than that of a hunting dog, will not need, and deserve, plenty of mental stimulation and exercise.

Even among the larger dogs, you have more significant differences than one normally thinks about. If you are interested in a Rhodesian Ridgeback, you need to be aware that the breed is very energetic and very

demanding, even as a 4-6 week-old puppy, and this tendency increases after the eight-week milestone, when the puppy is ready to leave his dam and go to a new owner. I have come across skilled breeders who have had litters of Golden Retrievers and Ridgebacks at the same time. After a few weeks, the need for the Retriever puppies to rest and sleep has forced the breeders to separate the litters, as the energy and intensity of play of the Ridgebacks was too much for the Golden Retrievers.

There are also some other, practical, considerations to take into account about a Ridgeback. It is short-haired, but these hairs stick to almost everything, so do not think that, as a short-coated breed, it will be easier to look after. Then, there is the big issue of physical and mental activity. A Ridgeback needs a few hours of free mobility, or at least some free mobility, and a lot – I mean a lot – of walking every day.

So, you have said "Yes" to all the questions? You understand what you are taking on and you have made an informed decision. You still want to buy a Ridgeback. Welcome to the happy gang. We will enjoy your company.

## WHICH SEX?

Now, male or female? I will leave this up to you. In the Ridgeback, the sex-driven characteristics are rather marked. The bitch exhibits more evidence of the 'wild dog', in her role as the hunter and the mother. She is also likely to come up with an endless supply of mischievous behaviour and wild adventures. The male is more stable in temperament from day to day. He is the real companion, the solid guardian, the 'guy to go out for a beer with' – do not take me too literally! When it comes down to it, the dog will mirror your interests and, with a breed as alert and quick to learn as the Ridgeback, you will be responsible for forming the relationship with your friend, be your chosen dog male or female. But please remember that it takes two to make and maintain that relationship.

## PURELY A PET

So, you want your Ridgeback to be 'just a pet', you said, or a healthy dog to keep on the farm for security and protection. You do not need a show dog. That is fine, but do remember that dog shows are competitions of sound breeding, not beauty contests, so

*The bitch exhibits something of the 'wild dog' in her moods and her behaviour can be wonderfully exciting on her terms.*

*The male is more stable in temperament and has the makings of a steady and predictable companion.*
*Photo: O. Rosenquist.*

you should avoid buying a puppy whose parents have no merit for showing purposes if this is due to major conformation or health faults. If you have really made up your mind that your Ridgeback will be a pet only, you can even take a dog with a faulty ridge I do not recommend you to do so, but the puppy will not suffer. However, you just need to make sure the dog will never, accidentally or otherwise, be used for breeding purposes.

*The temperament of the mother will be a good guide in assessing how the puppies will turn out.*

### SHOW POTENTIAL

To my mind, a dog with show potential is what you should go for. Read me correctly. I did not say a dog for show purposes, neither did I suggest you take up showing. Nobody, the world's most renowned breeders included, can give a 100 per cent guarantee that a puppy will develop into a winning show dog. The point is, it is best to go for a puppy which has no major faults, such as colour deviations, or already noticeable conformation problems.

It is possible that you might become interested in breeding in the future, and almost inevitably you will attend some shows. For this reason, before you choose your puppy, spend some time doing your homework. Your kennel club or national Ridgeback Club will advise you of suitable special books and publications that are worth reading. Then, buy the dog magazines and study the show results. The sign of a really good show dog is consistency. Not even the superstars of the dog world win at all the shows, so you need a broad base. When available, as is the practice in Germany and Scandinavia, read the judges' critiques. Note if one of the parents of the litter you consider buying from has a consistently mentioned physical fault. Then, visit several breeders and spend some time with the parents, getting to know their temperaments. Also, do go along to some shows and talk to people around the ring. Listen and ask questions, and learn to be critical. Naturally, breeders advertise their own bloodlines, but remember, even if you encounter some real 'salesmen' their claims are not necessarily incorrect, just truth told with a bit of fantasy.

Stay away from changing fashions in 'types'. There have been, and there will be, periods when rather extreme individuals receive praise and win a few classes at shows, but, if these 'types' are deviations from the Breed Standard, or extremes, they should be avoided. Recently there has been a tendency towards 'the more elegant type', for which you can read slimmer, thinner, cosmetically more elegant

*The breeder will help you to evaluate the litter, and will indicate those with anticipated show potential.*

Ridgebacks, almost greyhound-like. These are just fashions that come and go, as were the very large versions one saw some decades ago in a number of countries. I have a solid belief in the wisdom and persuasive power of 'back to basics', back to Africa, back to balance, back to functionality.

## WHO IS BOSS?

I have already mentioned that the Ridgeback puppy is very demanding and has a need for constant physical and mental exercise which increases as he grows up.

The most significant factor of all is that we are dealing with a very 'natural' breed, which I like to refer to as 'a basic dog'. The natural instincts and behavioural patterns of the wild dog are strong in a Ridgeback. This is an advantage if you can read dog signals, but it can become a problem if you are not consistent in your approach to, and training of, the adolescent Ridgeback.

I know of a case, in which a young family did not dare to enter their own bedroom after three months as Ridgeback owners. The five-month-old puppy was sitting on the bed, growling,

*The Ridgeback must learn to accept his subservient role in the human pack.*

'dangerously'. The family had allowed the puppy to take over as the leader of the pack, and the leader had chosen their bed as its 'sacred territory'. One cannot say Ridgebacks have bad taste, for the puppy had taken over the most comfortable part of the territory he commanded.

This story ended happily: the puppy was re-homed with new owners, who took command, gently and with understanding, and the puppy grew up to be a pleasant, obedient Ridgeback, who knew his place.

## TIPS FOR A NEW OWNER

My recommendation to all Ridgeback owners is to read as many books and articles about the breed as you can, or take a course in 'canine language'. The signal system of the basic canine – for instance a wolf – is clear, predictable and still very much present in a natural breed such as a Ridgeback.

The first ten months of your puppy's life in his new environment are the decisive ones. This is when you have the opportunity to form a sound relationship with your new family member – or create long-term problems.

Let us first establish three imperative rules about Ridgebacks and their training:

• Your dog will need to know the house rules, and later to develop the wish to work with you. The Ridgeback will never be an 'obedient dog' in the old sense, a marionette that blindly follows orders. If you wish your orders to be obeyed without question and in detail, you should consider owning another breed.

• The first seven to twelve months of a Ridgeback's life is when he must learn to live with you, and with your rules. But this is not the time to start teaching him more complicated issues such as competitive obedience training. His early months are when you should ideally be teaching him through play. 'Fun' is very much the key word during this period.

• Modern dog psychology accepts that breeds are different, and that individuals within the same breed have different characteristics. It is up to the owner/trainer to adapt techniques and sometimes even expectations, so that he does not try to force his dog into a rigid system at the expense of the animal's own individuality.

## EARLY DAYS

The first few days in his new home are in many ways the most decisive for any puppy. This is when good, and bad, habits are formed. For instance, make it clear

*The puppy has much to learn when he arrives in his new home.*

which are 'no-go' areas in the house. Choose these at the start, and be consistent. If you decide that the bedroom and library are forbidden territory for instance, do not allow the puppy in. Do remember to use a simple command – always the same one, and used by all family members – such as "No". When he approaches the door of the room, turn the puppy around gently, ideally by distracting his attention with something else. Do not compromise; any wavering will be noted by the puppy immediately, and be remembered.

If the puppy cries during the first nights with you, I suggest you do not take him into your bed, or onto the sofa, unless you want a nice 35-40 kg bedfellow in a year's time. Give him his own place where he is to sleep, with an old-fashioned "tick-tock" alarm clock to listen to, and be prepared to lose some sleep for the first few nights. It will pay off in the long term. The good old advice that a nice basket is a cosy home for a little puppy is always worth repeating.

Let the dog make a mental map of his territory. The quicker a puppy dares to sniff about and learn his way around, the more outgoing he will be. Remember to accompany the puppy and keep him away from the 'no-go' areas.

## PUPPY TALK

Start communicating with your puppy. As with all communication, what matters is not what you think you have said or signalled, but what has been experienced at the receiving end. Your body language and your facial expressions are stronger communicators than your voice. Keep your voice controlled, your body signals easy to read and do stay calm. Remember that leadership is not a question of who can shout the loudest, but of who deserves to be followed.

Your puppy wants, and needs, the stability and reassurance of a strict social pattern, which, if correctly instituted from the start, is all to your advantage. Establish early on that you and the other family members are the leaders of the pack. However, take care that you do not force the older puppy to try to accept a young child as a leader. Their relationship will create fewer problems if they are friends on more equal terms.

In the early stages you 'solve problems' for your puppy by providing food, shelter, and comfort. By giving him praise when he does as you want, you establish your position as the leader, without whom the puppy would have a hard time. Later on, you can move gradually toward letting the puppy solve his own problems – be it as simple as untangling himself when his leash has twisted around a tree – and give praise when the problem is solved.

Then come two parallel points that sometimes can create a conflict. You need to teach the dog to stay alone in his home. To begin with, leave him for very short periods, and gradually extend them. I recommend the same method when your dog must stay alone in the car. At the same time, be careful to notice any signals that the dog is getting bored. As I have said before, a Ridgeback does need a lot of mental stimulation. When playing with your puppy remember not to repeat any stimulation or any training moment too many times. A Ridgeback has a short attention span and can easily reject 'nagging', both vocal and physical.

Some of the stimulation can also be part of the puppy's education, as in the 'problem-solving' aspect of the game 'under which upside down cup is the little goodie?' – a simple game that keeps the puppy active and trains his use of the senses. Sometimes he can follow where you have hidden the tidbit with his eyes, sometimes he must use his nose.

## SOCIALISING

Allow the puppy to socialise by letting him meet other dogs and people, in a normal social setting. Social behaviour develops very early, so for his own safety the puppy should have the opportunity to learn dog language from adult dogs and to learn to respect bigger and stronger dogs. He will also pick up the correct canine signal systems to enable him to fit into the 'dog society' in your neighbourhood. The same rule applies with people – make sure the dog gets used to people as 'nice elements' within his world, so he does not develop any insecurity.

Be very alert when you present your puppy to young children. Do not allow the puppy to indulge in rough play with children, because two bad habits can develop. If the puppy is allowed to play by, for instance, dragging clothes, he can easily frighten a small child, leaving them scared of dogs. In contrast, I always say that dogs are frequently nicer to children than children are to puppies, so you must never, ever allow a child to behave badly towards a puppy (or, for that matter, any living creature). This rule applies to your own children, and to visitors. By taking on a puppy you have made the commitment, and equal terms must prevail with mutual fairness as the rule.

## TRAINING TO SHOW

Finally, assuming you are one of the readers who has considered the possibility of showing your dog one day, you need to train the puppy in the art of showing. This is not accomplished by dragging the puppy around an imaginary ring, but by getting him used to being handled and touched. When friends are visiting your home, ask

*A programme of socialisation is vital when rearing a young dog.*

them gently to have a quick glance at the puppy's teeth and to handle him a bit. Then, give the puppy a tidbit.

Never make a show debut at a big show. Ideally, start at a small outdoor event and make very, very sure the puppy has fun. A dog whose first experiences of the show environment are as something negative, or even just boring, will never be a big winner, even if he has next-to-perfect conformation. Some countries have 'mentality tests' for certain breeds, including Ridgebacks, so, as the owner, you should give some thought to this in good time. Watch a test, and understand it. In almost all cases, what we see is not so much 'mentality testing' as 'trainability testing'. Start getting your puppy prepared for the test by training him under positive circumstances. In my opinion these mandatory tests are unfortunate, as are most mandatory things in life, but they are the rules, and the rules must be obeyed.

Then, again, if you find your local kennel clubs or breed groups are offering professional mentality

description work, enter the tests. It is important, perhaps even more so for the owner than the dog, that one understands the true behavioural pattern of the breed.

## PUPPY TRAINING

For more detailed information about training of the puppy I recommend you read some of the specialist books on the subject, but here are a number of hints and suggestions as a start:

• Bring up your dog with a mixture of love and rules. The more positive emotions he feels, the happier the puppy will be but, for a dog, a life without rules decreases his feeling of security. Rules should be enforced from the

Bring your puppy up with a mixture of love and rules.

start, but rigid disciplinary training must not begin too early.

• The entire family must use the same signals, say the same words, and agree upon approved, as well as forbidden, territories in your home.

• Do not forget to mix 'stay with me' with some freedom. Dogs that do not experience enough freedom in the early days sometimes become 'runners-away' when they are grown up.

• Use soft and gentle hand signals. For instance, when pushing down the rump of your pup as you say "Sit", when you want to train him to sit down, do not keep it pressed down by force, or the command will become a negative experience.

• Before starting gradual training with a leash, give the puppy enough time to get used to the collar. Do not force the puppy to follow by your side. Just get him used to moving about on a leash. If he pulls, give gentle signals, but never drag him in by force. Again, following you must be a positive emotion.

• Teach the puppy to come back from an 'adventure' by a voice signal. The Ridgeback is a hunting dog, and, for his own safety, there will be instances when you will need to be able to call him in, even from a chase. Do not run after a puppy that is off on his own excursion. Wait until he looks at you, take a few steps away from the puppy, and then give your signal. Take your time, and remember to reward your puppy when he does come back.

• Do not expect too much from your puppy. The best results are obtained with a puppy that knows your basic rules but remains curious, alert, extrovert and happy.

*A well-behaved dog is a joy to own.*

# 4 *Training Your Ridgeback*

When I refer to an adult Ridgeback, I count from somewhere around 12 months, but this does not mean that a dog of this age is fully matured. A female Ridgeback matures, both physically and mentally, somewhere between 18 months and over two years, whereas a male seldom completes his growth or maturing process until around the age of three years. The Ridgeback is normally approaching final adult height at 9-12 months for females, and a little later for males, but they continue to grow in stature and substance. I want to make it clear that any sound dog will grow to the height he is genetically programmed for without over-feeding, or the use of high protein dog food. Natural growth should be allowed to take its time.

## TYPICAL BEHAVIOUR
Before I offer any advice on training – I will leave the more delicate task of training a future obedience show dog to specialist books and obedience classes – I will make some observations about Ridgeback behaviour. The understanding, on a scientific basis, of breed-specific behaviour is still in its infancy. Interesting research was pioneered by Hart, Murray, Hahs, Cruz and Miller in their paper Breed-Specific Behavioural Profiles of Dogs: Model for a Quantitive Analysis, University of Pennsylvania Press, 1983 (I recommend this collection of papers to every serious dog lover). One of the motivations for that study was predictability in the adult dog. The study included such elements as 'Ranking of Excitability', 'Ranking of Value as Watchdog', and 'Ease of House Training'. The most excitable was found to be the Fox Terrier, followed by the West Highland White Terrier and the Schnauzer, while the Schnauzer topped the watchdog list ahead of the West

*The Ridgeback is a highly intelligent breed, and its behaviour does not necessarily fit in with conventional patterns.*

Highland White Terrier and the Scottish Terrier. Ridgebacks have not, to my knowledge, been tested with such scientific thoroughness.

A classic remark, and one I have experienced when taking Ridgebacks through standard character tests is: "This (Ridgeback) behaviour does not fit into the pattern." My answer would normally be: "So, he is a typical Ridgeback." (The Swedish Kennel Club had a simple form, called 'Mentality Test', which, for a number of years was an obligatory prerequisite for Swedish championships. After thorough evaluation it was abandoned, as it added nothing to the cynological development.)

Excitability and fighting spirit are both characteristics that can be attributed to a Ridgeback. Give them the space to play, have fun, rip clothes between themselves, and they will have a field day. But do not try to excite them with something unexciting. They are likely to look at it, look at you, and say "No danger. What am I supposed to do with this (...piece of cloth etc.)?"

Another salutary lesson comes from Denmark, where a Ridgeback was doing exceptionally well, with an exceptional owner, in military police training. The only problem came when the Ridgeback was commanded to attack a padded arm or leg. It looked at it, thought "That won't have enough effect", and went for the unprotected extremity.

I will mention games and sports such as coursing a little later. The concept of lure coursing is for a dog to follow a teaser, normally a fast-moving plastic bag, as exactly and as fast as possible. I saw professional lure coursing for the first time in the US in 1986, where I had many good laughs, as well as valuable education. Some Ridgebacks had a chance to see the lure or teaser, in this case a plastic bag, in advance. So they looked at it flying away, looked at the handler, and clearly thought "No big loss." One or two did the full run, only to realise the coursing track started and ended with parallel straights where the courses met. So, the second time, they ran to the end of the parallel straight, stopped, and waited for the lure to come round the track and caught it from the front, on its return.

The most breed-significant element is, normally, the way in which the Ridgeback reacts to deliberate 'threats'. During testing or training, metal is sometimes used to create noises; in other sessions, umbrellas are flashed towards the dog, accompanied by voices and screams. The natural Ridgeback behaviour is to back away and move to the side instantly – just enough to be sure he or she would be outside an immediate danger zone. The Ridgeback then, typically, returns via a semi-circular motion, being prepared to hit back from the side, from behind, or from any angle typical for the breed. It cannot be stresssted too often: the true Ridgeback is not a 'head-on' attacker.

I can add another aspect of typical Ridgeback behaviour,

which is a true anecdote. One winter night, with snow falling, my very first male judged a group of noisy, somewhat pushy, youngsters as a risk. My dog was somewhat uncertain, not about his abilities, but about mine. So he kept me back firmly with a swift body movement, then disappeared into the snow, beyond the light shed by a nearby lamppost, only to re-appear from the other side, just showing his head and teeth in the light of the lamp. Needless to say, I was in no danger after that, just alone in the snow with a Ridgeback. Repeating such a test a few times normally produces a different pattern. The Ridgeback stops, says to himself "I've seen this before", yawns and demonstrates total boredom. The ability not to go head-on into danger is one of the most typical features of true Ridgeback behaviour. Another is to greet strangers without emotion, showing neither fear, aggression, nor even that much interest. A third talent is the ability to discern reality from artificial situations.

This very typical behaviour has also been interpreted as a lack of fighting spirit in today's Ridgebacks. The Megginson family (of the RR Club of

# TRAINING YOUR RIDGEBACK

Transvaal, South Africa), among others, have made tests with 'lap Ridgebacks' (who, I am told, even preferred sleeping in their bed), in front of cameras, where their dogs met real wild beasts for the first time. The dogs' reactions were spot-on. They were evasive, alert, courageous and still clever.

The long-standing chairman and secretary of the 'parent club' in Harare, Zimbabwe, keep reminding people of a true tale about a Ridgeback who got lost from a car in the Zimbabwean wilderness. The dog spent weeks and weeks in the bush, but finally was found and brought home, and such was his physical condition that he went on to win Best of Breed at his next show. He had no problems finding enough food in the wilderness!

I hope these stories will give you an idea of what to expect and what not to expect from your Ridgeback. Remember that, in a young dog, all these features, of caution and smartness, avoidance of danger etc., are accentuated. This, in combination with a short attention span, and his on-going interest in everything that is new, not old, gives you a platform from which you need to start your training work.

There is no need to train your Ridgeback to be a guard, this is part of his genetic make-up.

**GUARDING**
There is no need to train your young Ridgeback to be a guard dog, as he already has the talent for this in his genetic make-up. A Ridgeback is a wonderful natural guardian, insofar as he is never naturally aggressive, nor does he have a tendency to attack or inflict damage, unless absolutely necessary. So let the young dog learn to live normally within your family, which is the only introduction to guarding that you need to give a Ridgeback.

**WORDS OF WISDOM**
Training of the basics is easier if one remembers a number of old dog truisms:

43

• The balance between training alone, and training in groups with other dogs, is very important. With a Ridgeback, which is rather easily distracted as a young dog – that eternal curiosity again – I would suggest that you begin with some basic training alone at home, before joining a group or class. The advantage of going to a class later on is that the dog learns to concentrate, and to disregard outside disturbances.

• Try to practise training in different locations. A dog learns to obey your wishes by means of vocal commands and by your body language, by you giving the signals, and by the location. In an ideal situation you are better off if you train in at least three different locations.

• A dog forgets, just as human beings do. Do not take his apparent refusal to obey a command as stubbornness, or even stupidity. Keep your patience, and continue the training.

• A Ridgeback, as I have said before, needs several short training periods, rather than lengthy repetition of the same exercise. Stop the training for a period of play quite often to let the young dog relax. You might frequently find the Ridgeback is better off learning one thing, then having a period of play, before continuing the training on a different issue. Then give him a period of play again, and return to the original training exercise.

By the time your Ridgeback has reached adulthood, so should your relationship with your dog have developed and come of age. You know him, and he knows you and your family. He respects you as the pack leader. He thinks you, and the rest of the family, are fun, and he is happy when he is with you. You have worked out a basic routine so that you know what your Ridgeback needs in terms of exercise, both mentally and physically. You have basic control over the dog, i.e. he follows you on a leash and reasonably well without; you can call him to you when necessary, and you can prevent him from engaging in fights with threatening, over-dominant dogs, if need be.

## FIGHTING

At this stage, if not before, I am often asked the question: "What do I do if my Ridgeback is attacked by another big dog?" Firstly, I assume your Ridgeback has been exposed to other dogs, both older and younger, during his puppyhood and adolescence. He is confident of his, and other dogs', signalling systems. If your dog is loose and he, or she, meets another dog of the same sex, who is giving out clear signals of dominance or submission, do not get involved. If the situation is going on too long, or getting out of hand, then call your dog back to you.

If your Ridgeback meets a dog and the signals are predominantly those of aggression, not dominance (there is a difference!), try to call-in your dog at once, as long as this does not leave your

dog unnecessarily exposed. The reality of dog fights is that most are 'more talk than damage', but they can also develop into very dangerous situations. Do everything you can to avoid these, and never, ever, encourage a dog fight particularly involving a Ridgeback, even with the idea that he has to 'learn a little'. You own one of the fastest, smartest and toughest canines on earth. Also, you own a Ridgeback, a breed that in every part of the world which knows anything about dog breeds, is considered a socially acceptable, nice-natured breed. No-one has the right to jeopardise the acceptability and the honour

*If you learn to read your dog's body language, you will be able to tell whether his intentions are aggressive or not. Here, the Doberman clearly signals submission.*

of our breed by having his Ridgeback play rough. If the unfortunate situation occurs that your dog is, involuntarily, involved in a bad fight, get the nearest person you trust to co-operate with you, both grabbing both back legs of each dog at the same time, pulling them apart. This works, every time. No dog can bite when its hind legs are being held.

## ON YOUR BIKE

It is most important to find ways of stimulating your Ridgeback in his day-to-day life. To date, I have never met a Ridgeback that does not like running alongside you when you ride a bike. If you have a chance to ride, let your dog run beside your horse a few times a week.

If you are going to start cycling with your Ridgeback, take a few words of advice from someone who has learned by his mistakes for over 20 years. Buy a substantial bicycle with foot brakes, though a hand brake, for your right hand, with the dog running on your left, gives added security. Do not take your dog cycling until he can walk properly on a leash, obeying the basic commands. Also, from a strictly

physiological point of view, I suggest you never start cycling with, or over-exercising, a Ridgeback in any other way, before his joints and muscles are well established at approximately two years of age.

Use a double-leash, i.e. one you can twist securely around your left hand, and use a glove, at least on your left hand. To begin with, until your dog has got used to the consequences of turning too fast (especially turning right, when the dog can hit the front wheel), use a fairly short leash. Do not use a dog harness, of the type designed for pulling a sledge, unless you are as strong as Arnold Schwartzenegger and have the massive strength in your left hand to slow your Ridgeback down when he wants to speed up, and then turn around, stop etc.

I have had many light-hearted moments when cycling with my Ridgebacks, but there are some risks. I have overtaken mopeds (50cc junior motorbikes) travelling at the legal limit when being pulled along by a male Ridgeback – without me even pedalling! Some Ridgebacks do want to gallop along at full speed, just to use up their surplus energy and this is when things become tricky. Others, perhaps with more freedom to work off their excitement at home, just love the long, steady runs with their masters. My first Ridgeback male ran up to 20 kilometres a day. The beauty of the steady run is that your Ridgeback will refine his trot to perfection, assuming his conformation is correct, and he gets used to trotting at speed, without accelerating into a gallop. This is how a Ridgeback shows himself at his very best in a show ring.

## BASIC COMMANDS

A few words about the most essential training objectives: *Teaching your Ridgeback to sit.*

Start by remembering that:
• you need to give the physical and verbal commands simultaneously.
• any praise must come when the performance is correct, i.e. the dog is really sitting.

Begin by placing the collar forward, under the lower jaw and close to the ear, and keep the leash in your right hand. As you give the rump of the dog a gentle push downwards, at the same time firmly, but without rushing, pull the leash backwards and slightly

upwards. The order of events is: Start saying "Sit" i.e. "Sii...(push with left hand, pull leash with right hand)..itt!"

When your dog sits for a few seconds give him praise, and possibly a little tidbit. Take care here, as he might learn to stand up. Or, seeing the tidbit waiting in your hand, he may not remain parallel to you but will turn towards you.

Never be late giving praise, so that you are still saying "Good boy" after the dog has stood up, or he will learn that 'sitting is a bit boring but getting up is fun and my master is pleased with me too'.

*Note: Never, ever, hit the dog on the rump. This signals nothing but punishment, but is not associated with any performance or wrong-doing.*

*Walking on a leash – without pulling*
In today's society chances to let your dog run free, even in the countryside, are pitifully scarce. Hence, you should teach your dog to walk on a leash, 'half-free', giving him a chance to experience some freedom, sniff around and investigate, without pulling. In this training exercise no vocal command is used.

Use a long, soft leash. Allow your dog to choose the main direction he wants to move in, giving him some sense of freedom. If the dog pulls, lift your hand with the leash taut, then move it forward to loosen the leash for a fraction of a second and move your hand down and back in a fast movement, as if you were shaking dust from a carpet. This creates a strong momentary sensation in the collar, which the dog associates with the pulling.  Say nothing, but if the dog stops pulling, move alongside him and praise him while he is not pulling. Repeat, with silence and patience, every time you walk your young dog.

*Calling in your dog*
This is possibly the most important command for your dog to know. It can save you from social embarrassments, but more importantly, it can save your Ridgeback from traffic and other accidents.

First of all, start with a long, soft leash. When your dog is not watching you, pull sharply and firmly on the leash while giving the command "Here" (or whatever the message is in your language). Make sure your dog does not see you manoeuvre the leash, or you risk that he feels coming to you is unpleasant. When you have sent your signal by pulling, and the dog has started to move towards you, do two things. Move back a few steps, still keeping the leash loose, and keep praising your dog as long as he moves towards you. Backing up like this gives the dog an impression of moving over a longer distance. It also links to your training during his puppy stage, when you moved away from him when you wanted him to run towards you.

This training can easily become monotonous, which is why you can keep your Ridgeback alert by varying the theme, while still strengthening the dog's wish to come to you. When you have reached the level that you can train without a leash, play hide-and-seek; let the dog search, find and come to you. Give him plenty of praise and some tidbits.

It is imperative to make sure, when you train without a leash, that you are in an area that is fenced in. There must be no traffic around the training area. A rabbit, another dog, or a cat, is all that is needed for the young dog to run off, which could be disastrous if there are cars around. In order to

*Choose a distraction-free area when you start training without a leash.*

reinforce the necessity to come to the master when called, you can use the opportunity when your dog does not obey you to disappear for a while. Make him worried, then show yourself, call "Here", and praise him when he arrives.

The training exercise to bring your Ridgeback to you when called needs more, and then more, repetition, over at least two months. Then test your dog by taking him for walks in the forest, or in fenced areas with other dogs, making sure you can command your Ridgeback by your voice.

Also practise calling him back when he is interested in chasing something or having great fun.

## SPORTS
When you have taught your dog the basic commands, it is up to you to decide if you want to continue, when your Ridgeback is a young adult, with more advanced and serious obedience training. Obedience training, correctly taught, and remembering you have a Ridgeback, not a German Shepherd, is also fun for the dog.

While your Ridgeback is young,

decide on other types of activity that you want to choose to keep him active, and that will give you a chance to spend some quality time with your dog.

## AGILITY

This sport is 'Obstacle Grand Prix', or showjumping with a dog. The modern version, parallel agility, where two dogs are matched against each other to see who clears all obstacles in the fastest time, is the dog sport of the future.

I also foresee that this is going to be a major TV sport before long. But, what is even better, this is something a Ridgeback really loves and can excel at. His problem is over-enthusiasm, so have patience, and he will, rest assured, be among the fastest, once he has grasped the idea and understands the rules. But he might sometimes fail to take it seriously and jump a few of the obstacles twice – just for fun.

## COURSING

Coursing is a combination of greyhound racing, i.e. chasing a lure attached to a fast-moving cable, and motocross, i.e. driving cross-country.

Whether your country arranges the US 'long-track' version or the slightly more artificial, but more exciting – from a spectator standpoint – 'Australian short-track' version, do try it.

The original concept of US Lure

*Ridgebacks excel at Agility and other action filled canine sports – although a degree of over-enthusiasm may have to be curbed.*

*Coursing is becoming a popular sport among Ridgeback owners.*

Coursing is to lay, in a natural setting, a track that looks as close as possible to the classic escape pattern of a hare. Fast straight out, demanding zigzag movements, some very hard 90 degree turns, and then the final life-saving fast straight.

What could suit a Ridgeback better, at least for fun?

*Note: If, and when, you do try Lure-Coursing with your Ridgeback, which I warmly recommend, remember to reinforce your calling-back training quite frequently, so the fun of the game does not overshadow the discipline to return to the owner on command.*

## DOG SHOWS

Possibly less fun for your dog than either of the above sports, but this is most essential in the long term to promote sound dog breeding.

Showing a Ridgeback follows on naturally from the comments about physical exercise. We agreed, when talking about the young puppy, that all showing must be fun for the dog, or he will never exhibit all his best qualities. So, hopefully, you will have started with some small shows, making triple sure the dog enjoyed the outing. The show placing of a puppy is not important. Puppy shows should be fun, fun, training, and more fun. Bringing in a strong element of competitiveness is unfair to the dog and frequently disheartening to the owner. Basically, I am against all kinds of bans and over-regulation by kennel or Ridgeback clubs, but I have made representations against the results

*It is the dogs that win in the show ring that will generally be used for breeding, and so dog showing has long-term implications for each breed.*

from puppy shows being used in the advertising of stud dogs. This is how I think one should view a dog show:

• It is a contest of sound breeding, where you get expert judges' opinions about individual dogs. These opinions have a use when evaluating the breeding qualities of individual dogs (they are not the only criteria), and the critiques are also of major importance when assessing quality trends, on a broader scale, of given dog breeds.

• Success, or the lack of it, in the show ring does not change the value of a dog, and it should never reflect on your close and warm relationship with your good companion.

• Your task in the show is, by correct and just means, to show the strengths of your dog as best you can. No-one should expect you to highlight the weaker points (and, as with humans, there are no totally faultless individuals). This means you must understand the dog breed and its Standard, and you must have an objective picture of your own dog when showing him.

• Showing a dog should be treated as a sport. It is neither the most important thing in life nor the end of the world if you have a bad day. But the judge and the breed deserves that you train your dog properly for showing, and you do your best every time you

*Assessing ridges in the show ring.*

decide to enter a show. It also means you should consider your dog as a sportsman. He or she must be in peak condition on the day of the show.

• Finally, showing is a subjective sport, so do not expect the results to be identical at each show. The judge does not have a bad memory if he places an identical group of dogs in different orders on different occasions. Showing means competing with the dog according to his condition on the day, taking into account your handling work in the ring – and that will vary considerably as well – and basing the results on the few minutes the judge sees each dog on that particular occasion.

## PREPARING FOR THE SHOW

There are a few points to keep in mind when planning for a show. I will take it for granted that your dog's vaccinations are up to date, you have filled in the entry forms, and collected all his documents together ready for the trip. Getting these things organised in good time should ensure that the day gets off to a good start.

Remember that the show atmosphere is both a physical and mental strain. Have a sufficiently large water bowl filled with fresh

water for your dog at all times, and take a suitable piece of carpet, Vetbed, or blankets for your dog to lie on. If it is an outside show, you will also need some plastic sheet to put under the carpet. Ridgebacks are short-haired dogs but they also have a tendency to

*Dog showing is a sport that can be enjoyed by all the family.*

become little prima donnas at shows, so some extra pampering will not come amiss. Invest in a special show set of a collar and a rather short leash. The dog soon learns to understand the importance of changing to the 'show gear'.

Dress appropriately, either in smart casual wear or quality sportswear which are nowadays just as acceptable as more formal dressing. Remember to wear comfortable and practical shoes that you can run well in!

Following the dress code is a courtesy to the judge and the officials in the ring, and behind the scenes, and it also reflects, in the eyes of spectators, on the breed you are showing. Every time you show a Ridgeback you are an ambassador for the breed.

Learning how to show your dog is ultimately up to you. You need to develop your own style, based very much upon the strengths and weaknesses, and the temperament, of your Ridgeback. Watch the experienced handlers at work and try adopting their 'tricks' and techniques when you are practising, adapting them to suit you, but in the end it is you and your dog in the ring, nobody else. Ultimately it is a question of you and your dog understanding each other, working together and enjoying the co-operation!

Just one final piece of advice on showing. If you do not win, congratulate the winner with warmth. If you do win, accept the congratulations of your competitors with grace, but do not feel let down if you are placed second the next time you show. Classes won are victories for ever, and later losses do not tarnish the shine of the good results!

# Breeding
# Ridgebacks

Breeding is a magical experience. Seeing new representatives of the breed being born is an unforgettable feeling for any dog lover. At the same time, breeding changes your role in the game of responsibility, for you are now answerable for future generations of the breed.

## SHOULD YOU BREED?

There are a number of criteria for dogs that can, and should, be bred from, and for ones that should not. A responsible owner should never breed from dogs which show any of the following defects.

• Ridgeless Ridgebacks, or individuals with severe ridge

*If you to breed from your bitch, you must take on a burden of responsibility – from finding the optimum combination to screening the puppy buyers.*

problems, must not be used.

• Individuals who have suffered from Dermoid Sinus, even if they have been operated on successfully should also be excluded.

• Clearly, faulty colours such as silver, or excessive black or white, should disqualify a dog from a breeding plan.

• Severe functional faults caused by incorrect conformation of the dog, such as being too short in the body, having serious front, or rear, angulatory problems, noticeably incorrect bites, the lack of several teeth, or a weak underjaw, must exclude a dog from breeding. So must an obvious kinked tail syndrome (especially if this is also apparent in parents and/or littermates). Missing teeth is a controversial subject. I can accept that if, for instance, only one tooth is missing, careful breeding could be possible if all progeny are carefully checked before the next litter. But missing teeth is a fault, and cannot be dismissed lightly.

• Avoid breeding from dogs with Hip Dysplasia. However, on this point I hold controversial views. I can see reasons why exceptions could be made, but only in rare cases, and for particular reasons. A Ridgeback that has unique

qualities, perhaps in shape of body and/or head, which is possibly being lost in a particular bloodline, could be used once, assuming that the HD score is not too serious. One would assume that both parents of the individual have correct HD scores. If such an exception is made, the dog or bitch should be used only once, with no possibility of another mating until the entire litter has had its HD scores confirmed by X-ray, at the minimum age of one year. And, naturally, that single breeding must be with an equally high-quality partner. I repeat that I accept exceptions for exceptional dogs – but these exceptions occur very rarely.

When you are a member of a breed club which has rules that are different from the above principles, the rules of your particular club must be followed.

On the issue of the responsibility of breeding from a sound Ridgeback, one which fulfils the above criteria, I also have a very clear viewpoint.

Only a fool does not ask for advice, and anyone who thinks he or she knows it all is merely showing their ignorance. So, talk, ask, read, talk more, ask for the opinions of as many experienced people as you possibly can. Then remember that, in the dog world, truth is normally a critical viewpoint based on the average of several expert opinions. Before you breed for the first time, I suggest you also have a discussion with your veterinary surgeon.

When you feel certain that you want to breed, and have identified for what reasons, and towards what target you are aiming, the final decision is yours. It is your dog, it is your vision, it is your dream, and it is, in the end, your responsibility.

## GENETICS

If you are keen to start breeding from your Ridgeback, I recommend that you read some first-rate books on genetics. There are a number of facts and aspects that show what to look for and what to learn more about.

Before you begin breeding, you have to understand the laws of genetics. There are some rules without exceptions – regarding the predisposition for the ridges or ridgelessness, for instance. Yet, at the same time, genetics are exceptionally complicated, and nature has an unrivalled skill in making exceptions.

You need to realise that a single parent's chromosomes can contain about 550 million different combinations – and that there are two parents to a combination!

A puppy gets 50 per cent of its genes from each of the two parents. If you go further back in the pedigrees, the grandparents give 25 per cent family relationship, but the decision from which grandparent certain qualities come is strictly a case of probability. For each characteristic that goes into the gene pair of a given quality, there are eight choices, when you count all four grandparents together, so grandparents have a clear influence, but the variation is by chance. And, going further back in the pedigree, hoping, for instance, to find a great 'star', is not necessarily fruitful.

The debate about whether you should go for dogs with show merit or not is presumably eternal. We have found that going further back in the pedigree than to grandparents gives a low probability of getting exactly any individual dog's qualities in any way, shape or form. On the other hand, even if we take into account the environmental factors that may have created a great champion, that dog has proved something, so

*The stud dog you choose must be sound in temperament and free of inherited diseases.*

it would be foolish not to consider a successful showdog. Then again, this does not by definition mean his, or her, littermates will have the same qualities.

Genetic make-up and environment go hand in hand to produce the final result. In modern breeding programmes the quality and the selectiveness of material, at least among the successful breeders, is normally so good that environment normally has as much influence on an individual dog's show potential as, or more than, his ancestry.

Most of the qualities we look for are also exceptionally complex, depending on a huge number of interrelated factors.

For genetic inheritance probabilities, the following frameworks are valid:

| | Inherited percentage |
|---|---|
| Birth weight | 20-45% |
| Size (height of dog etc.) | 40-85% |
| Fertility | 10-20% |
| Mental characteristics | 0-80% |

In order to evaluate the breeding quality of a male or bitch, by far the best measure is reproduction evaluation. This means, in layman's terms, making a systematic evaluation of the main qualities of all puppies produced by potential parent dogs. If you are the owner of a bitch and you are trying to decide whether to breed from her for the first time, this is, naturally, pure theory, but it is all the better a reason to choose a male that has already been proven.

The next best evaluation possibility is to judge the quality of the litters the parents were born into. An 'odd one out', unless signalling a hereditary defect, is normal, especially in a large litter.

The third method is pedigree evaluation. It has to be noted that you need expert opinions – or access to a computer programme of a modern kennel or breed club – to make any sense of a pedigree. Certainly, a large number of champions in a pedigree says something, i.e. the sheer statistical probability of faultless backgrounds increases, but what you really need is a listing of genetically-transmitted problems, such as ridgelessness, colour problems or skeletal problems, including kinked tails.

In addition, building your own 'data-bank' around interesting pedigrees is not all about hi-tech. Collect photos to give a pedigree a more useful life.

Over a period of time, you can develop a routine of making your own notes highlighting the qualities in pedigrees. In the end, *sound* breeding assumes the avoidance of introducing or duplicating faults, but *great* breeding can only be achieved when you have learnt to understand a dog's strengths.

If you are obsessed by finding faults, you will not move a breeding programme forward. Success is created by spotting superior strengths.

## GENETICS OF RIDGES

Let us use ridges, or the lack of them, as an example of genetic rules (the same rules apply in other breeds, for instance, in determining whether a puppy gets a short or a long tail). The possession of a ridge is a dominant characteristic. All genetic qualities are based upon gene pairs. There are two basic possibilities: 'even pairs' of genes, referred to as Homozygotes, or 'mixed pairs', Heterozygotes.

You have the two optional hereditary alternatives for the production of the ridge, the gene for ridge (let us call it R), or the genetic programming for ridgelessness (let us use rl as a

*The possession of a ridge is a dominant characteristic.*

symbol). That is, a single Ridgeback can carry the gene pairs for ridge (RR) or ridgelessness (rl rl), in both cases being homogenous or Homozygote; or the individual can carry a mixed gene, (R rl), being of Heterozygote character.

The use of capital letters "R" and lower case "rl" also signal another important factor: qualities, or characteristics, can either be 'dominant' or 'recessive', and it is common in genetics that dominant characteristics are marked with capitals and recessive with lower case. In simple terms, a dominant gene is higher in the genetic order than the recessive. The ridge must be a dominant characteristic. The original hair

formation on the back was a result of a mutation, and became the dominant characteristic for dogs with the mutated genes (just as short tails are dominant over long tails). Since the mutations took place naturally, long ago, it is also a hint about the geographical origin of ridged dogs. From the point of view of genetic probability, the ridge formation is more likely to have originated in Africa, as it has too limited a distribution in Asia.

It is also most likely, talking specifically about the ridge, that the original mutation concerned the growth direction of the hair on the back of the body, nothing more. It was either 'growing towards the back', as in all other

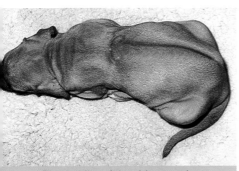

*The quality of the ridge can be assessed immediately after birth.*

dog breeds or 'growing forwards'. There is no mention of crowns in early records so it is a fair assumption that today's symmetric ridge is a result of systematic breeding, i.e. an acquired characteristic, not a result of a mutation. The whorls, nowadays referred to as crowns, are presumably a logical result of breeding a symmetric hair formation. On the body of any dog you can find many places where hair directions meet, forming borders, lines, or even whorls (as under the ears). In general, hair always grows in the direction on a particular part of the body that gives the optimal protection when the dog is in motion, so a dog, having many facets to his body, will have several changes of direction in the hair growth. Concequently on the

back, when the mutated signal for hair 'growing forwards' meets regular hair directions, the result has gradually been that a symmetry has developed into roundish whorls which mark the main turning point in the growth of the hair direction.

So how do genetics affect the ridge? Mathematics determines that you have a given number of possible combinations. Each parent has one of three gene pair alternatives:

R     R
R     rl

In these cases the individual carries a ridge.

rl     rl

In this case the individual is ridgeless.

Disregard if the male or female is shown on top or on the side of the 6 grids below, this is what happens in the various combinations.

| 1. | R | R |
|----|----|----|
| R | RR | RR |
| R | RR | RR |

Both parents of the Ridgeback puppy have homozygote, i.e. even pairs for having the characteristic of a ridge. Result: All puppies have ridges. All puppies carry homozygote gene pairs for ridge.

| 2. | R | rl |
|----|----|-----|
| R | RR | Rrl |
| R | RR | Rrl |

One of the parents has the homozygote gene pair for ridge, the other parent has a pair of heterozygote, or mixed, genes for ridge and ridgelessness. Both parents, naturally, have ridges. Result: All puppies have a ridge (remember that the gene for ridge was a dominant quality in a mixed gene pair). However, half of the puppies carry heterozygote gene pairs, that is, in the next generation if mated with a Ridgeback with heterozygote gene pairs (alternatively a homozygote gene pair for ridgelessness) you will have a number of puppies without ridges in that mating – See Table 3.

| 3. | R | rl |
|----|----|------|
| R | RR | Rrl |
| rl | Rrl | rlrl |

Both parents are heterozygote, that is they carry a ridge but also have a mixed gene with qualities for ridge as well as ridgelessness. Result: The relation between ridges and ridgeless puppies in the litter is 3 : 1. (50 per cent of the puppies have a ridge but are heterozygote, 25 per cent carry homozygote gene pair for ridgelessness. These 25 per cent are ridgeless, so in this combination you see the problem). Please note that the percentages are averages, not final formulae in single litters.

| 4. | rl | rl |
|----|-----|-----|
| R | Rrl | Rrl |
| R | Rrl | Rrl |

Note: This is a hypothetical or test mating only for a Ridgeback, as one of the parents does not carry a ridge. The other one is homozygote for ridge. Result: As the ridge gene is dominant, all puppies carry ridge but all are heterozygote. This is what must have happened in Africa, when the indigenous ridged dogs were mated to, for instance, European hunting dogs.

In this case, all the mixes between a ridged dog and a non-ridged breed carried ridges.

This genetic model also tells us that the ridge is dominant. There are many cases, almost all accidental, of breedings between Ridgebacks and other breeds. In these crossings there have been puppies carrying ridges. (If the ridge was a recessive characteristic, there would not have been ridged puppies in the first generation of this new crossbreed.)

| 5. | rl | rl |
|---|---|---|
| R | Rrl | Rrl |
| rl | rlrl | rlrl |

Another test – or picture of previous ages when dogs with ridge formations mated dogs without.

Result: The only combination in which 50 per cent of the puppies carry ridge. The ridged puppies are all heterozygote, the ridgeless logically homozygote for ridgelessness.

Playing with our theories on old Africa, as in No. 4, this would have been the result if the puppies of the, let's say African ridged dog and Pointer, mated another non-ridged dog. This outcome again proves that originally there must have been enough dogs in limited areas for early ridged dogs to remain ridged. Because the securing of ridged dogs rested on enough matings going back to 3, i.e. also providing homozygote individuals with ridges.

| 6. | rl | rl |
|---|---|---|
| rl | rlrl | rlrl |
| rl | rlrl | rlrl |

Just to complete the mathematical options. Two parents, both without ridge, i.e. homozygote for ridgelessness.

Result: All puppies ridgeless and all homozygote for ridgelessness.

When genetic rules suggest 75 per cent get ridge, it means three quarters on an accumulated average basis. Probability being what it is, it is possible that all puppies in a litter, especially a small litter, carry ridges! Seen from the standpoint of probability, the one quarter ridgeless have not been born. Statistically, this means that if a mating produces only ridged puppies, it is still theoretically possible that one of the parents is heterozygote.

Over time, repeating the mating many times, the proportions will near 3:1 in descendants. Naturally, it would not be impossible, though three times less likely, that all puppies in a small litter were ridgeless.

Alternative three is also the most surprising for many younger breeders, as you produce a characteristic, i.e. some ridgeless puppies, with two parents that visually are fully-fledged Ridgebacks.

In real life, there is only one way of making sure a male or female is homo- or heterozygote for ridge, i.e. carries full or mixed gene quality for ridge – test-mate the individual with one that has proved, in earlier matings, to be heterozygote (that is, it has produced ridgeless puppies). If the test litter only produces ridged dogs, it is likely, unless it is a very small litter, the new dog is homozygote for ridge. This test is fine in theory only, naturally, I would not recommend it in practice.

So, in summary, if a mating produces ridgeless puppies, the gene base for ridgelessness is always in both parents.

When talking about the key element of the breed, the ridge, it should be noted that the existence and placement of the two crowns must follow a more complex genetic formula, which is not fully understood today. It is common for 'half ridges' to occur, either to the left or right, with one crown and a partial arch. It is also not uncommon to have two 'half ridges', with one crown each and half an arch each, above each other, on the same side of the dog. This suggests the 'crown and arch' gene combinations come in halves. It is most unlikely that nature, genetically, regards a Ridgeback

with a hair formation, but without crowns, as ridgeless, but rather as a ridged individual. I do not encourage test breedings of this kind, but if the procedure is carried out correctly, and the puppies are not registered and sold for breeding purposes, I cannot condemn it either.

## ARRIVAL OF THE PUPPIES

Having puppies around is almost as demanding as having your own babies, and takes a great deal of time and care. The very first days and weeks of the newborn are most decisive for their future development. Thus, if you decide to have a litter and you own the bitch, make sure you, or someone, will have a chance to be with the litter on a regular basis for eight weeks. Taking one or two weeks off is not an option.

The puppies must have plenty of natural light. Being in the dark too much, as in a garage without windows, hampers their mental development. Choose an area as a nursery where the puppies are safe from electric wires etc. as their teeth grow faster than you think.

Build a 'puppy box', with minimum dimensions of 1.5 x 1.5 metres, from which the young pups cannot escape and which,

*The mother will care for all the puppies' needs in the first couple of weeks.*

later on, becomes their safe haven, where they can retreat for a rest between the play and mischief of their active periods. After a few days their mother will be glad of a place where she can escape, to rest and sleep alone for a little while. You can either have a slightly larger puppy box, with a raised area for the bitch which is beyond the reach of the puppies, or a separate sleeping area immediately outside the box.

The nursery needs to be kept at an even temperature, of around 20 degrees, day and night. Once the puppies begin to move around without too much effort, they are better off being allowed out into a much larger play area a few times per day.

Good hygiene is most important. You can buy effective, non-odour, non-toxic, disinfectants from the pharmacy. An old, but always good, piece of advice is to collect newspapers for a number of months before the birth, as these quickly become the natural 'toilet area' for the small puppies, and the papers are easy to remove and burn, replacing them with new fresh ones.

Once the puppies are big

*The puppies will divide their time between eating, sleeping and playing.*

enough to move around on – more or less – stable legs, make sure they have a water bowl available. Choose one with low sides, to prevent accidents should a puppy that might be weak or ill get stuck in the bowl.

Puppies need the chance to be outdoors. Hopefully in the sun, but that is difficult to get on demand!

Once they are 4-5 weeks old, it will be time to let potential buyers visit the puppies. Let the bitch meet them first, because this way you avoid her getting worried, but also because a Ridgeback mother has a super instinct towards people. I have never sold a puppy to a person the Ridgeback mother has signalled she does not like or trust. Puppies should never be handed over to their new homes before they have reached a minimum of 8 weeks of age.

The quality of the ridge can be assessed immediately after the birth. Asymmetric ridges or lack of them, or alternatively, too many crowns, will never change. After the first few days the ridges become blurred, but they return, and are easily visible, after a few weeks.

*As the puppies get older, potential buyers will come to inspect them.*

# 6

# *Health*
# *Issues*

This chapter makes no claims to be an ABC of health care for dogs, but what you will find are basic comments about nutrition; hereditary faults appearing at birth, i.e. ridgelessness, kinked tails, Dermoid Sinus, and Hip Dysplasia; first aid; inoculations; and care of the ageing dog.

## PUPPY NUTRITION

The most essential principle of puppy nutrition is to let the mother feed them for as long as possible. The first 3-4 weeks can well be left entirely to the bitch, after which a gradual education process can begin to introduce the puppies to other foods. It is a good habit to have the puppies fully weaned 7-12 days before they go to their new homes, which should never be before eight weeks of age.

If the mother has insufficient milk, or she has an illness, or if the

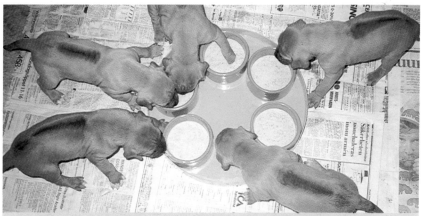

*Weaning is a gradual process, starting when the puppies are 3-4 weeks of age.*

litter is very big, you will need to consider substitutes for breast feeding from an early age. Compared to cow's milk consumed by human beings, the bitch's milk contains almost 100 per cent more dry matter, and more than double the proportions of fat and protein.

Pharmacies, or your veterinary surgery, can supply you with artificially produced milk substitutes. A much cheaper solution, if you have the time and patience, is to produce your own blend, which I suggest contains: 80 per cent cow's milk (3 per cent fat) and 20 per cent light cream (10-12 per cent fat).

For each litre of this mixture, add one egg yolk plus 6 grams of bone meal.

Puppies that are undernourished can be fed with a baby bottle. It is important to take your time and to keep the  puppy warm, especially the very young puppy. It also helps if you caress the puppy's belly while you feed him.

From the table below you can estimate the nutritional requirements of the puppies (it is easier if and when you have moved to manufactured food, as that gives you details of the exact nutritional value of the contents):

| Body Weight | Puppy /growth kcal | Adult kcal |
|---|---|---|
| 1 kg | 275 | |
| 2 kg | 470 | |
| 3 kg | 630 | |
| 4 kg | 770 | |
| 5 kg | 900 | |
| 6 kg | 1040 | |
| 7 kg | 1170 | |
| 8 kg | 1315 | |
| 9 kg | 1430 | |
| 10 kg | 1530 | |
| 15 kg | 2050 | |
| 20 kg | 2600 | |
| 25 kg | 3000 | 1500 |
| 30 kg | 3500 | 1700 |
| 35 kg | | 1900 |
| 40 kg | | 2100 |
| 45 kg | | 2300 |

*A useful average of contents as a percentage of adult dry food, is 90 per cent dry matter, 10 per cent water, with 22-24 per cent protein, 8 per cent fat, 1 per cent linoleic acid and 3-4 per cent fibres.*

There is an on-going debate about the need for nutritionally enhanced special food for growing puppies. My advice is to avoid puppy foods that are too 'strong', and definitely do not 'fortify' them further to make your puppy grow 'fast and strong'. A slow, even growth is better than too fast a growth.

If you have dietary or stomach problems with your youngsters, do not wait too long to check with a veterinarian. One reason is that illnesses, such as the ever-changing and very serious Parvovirus, need care early on. So, if your dog gets bad diarrhoea and/or shows other symptoms of being unwell, it is better to check with your vet than to wait.

## FEEDING THE ADULT

For the grown-up dog, less intense feeding is to be recommended if, for instance, due to travel or stress, the dog has a temporary stomach problem. It is worth remembering that lamb meat is gentler on the system, so the various lamb and rice diets on the market are worth trying in these cases.

However, if your dog is in training for energetic sports such as Lure Coursing, Agility or any

*The development of good bone and muscle is dependent on feeding a high-quality, balanced diet.*

other intensive physical exercise like hunting, and he loses weight, try him on a high-energy food which has a greater protein content. But you should only do this if he does use all that extra energy. If he loses weight suddenly, *always* consult your vet urgently.

Ridgebacks, as with any breed of dog, can develop pollen allergies, which could originate from their diet. If your Ridgeback loses the shine on his coat, starts losing his hair and begins to look in bad shape, change his food, and watch for any possible effects. I have seen this simple expedient bring about an improvement on many occasions.

## FIRST AID

As to general health issues, I firmly recommend that anyone who may want to become a breeder one day, takes a First Aid course to learn how to treat common diseases and deal with minor accidents.

Here are just a few of the basics:
• During the summer, if your dog is running free in a vulnerable area, you should have serum against snake bites available.
• Any dog, taken along on a sailing or motor boat, over any

long distance, should have a life-vest.
• Remember that first aid can be given to dogs in the same way as to human beings. For instance, a dog hurt in a traffic accident can be given mouth-to-muzzle artificial respiration.
• If your dog has swallowed something hard or sharp, never try to make him vomit, but take him immediately to the vet. The same rule applies if you know that your dog has swallowed some caustic acid.
• If, on the other hand, the dog has eaten dangerous amounts of expanding food, such as dry dog food, rotten meat, or an animal such as a rat or a squirrel, get him to vomit. The easiest way is to give him, every quarter of an hour, a mixture of a teaspoonful of salt in an equal amount of water. Pour it into his mouth and close the mouth by keeping your hands around the muzzle until the mixture has been swallowed.

## VACCINATIONS

Inoculations are a straightforward issue in most European countries. Your kennel club and veterinary authorities have issued clear regulations regarding vaccination against distemper and, in many cases, leptospirosis etc. Make sure that you have this information before you acquire your first dog, and also that you check any vaccination certificates you get from the breeder of your dog.

## HEREDITARY FAULTS

Hereditary faults must, from the very first sign, be noted down and openly communicated. Sound dog breeding – and a sound reputation in any dog or breed club – stems from openness and honesty. There is nothing to be ashamed of in registering faults. There is no breeder on earth who has not faced problems, but it is by hiding faults that do we do most damage to the breed.

If, as has, unfortunately, happened occasionally with Ridgebacks (and with all breeds, in all countries), a breeder tries to take advantage of another breeder's misfortune to indulge in a little negative publicity in order to gain an advantage, that is a case for disciplinary action within his own breed club.

## LACK OF RIDGE

Ridgelessness exists, and will continue to exist, in our breed. In the early days of the breed, ridged dogs were mated to ridgeless ones.

As we have seen, it is inevitable that some individuals carry the heterozygote or mixed gene pair, which combined with another heterozygote will give ridgeless puppies.

The kindest thing to do is to have ridgeless puppies in a litter put down. In a situation where registration or controlled de-registration is possible, the breeder can ensure that information about the litter goes into breed statistics, and at the same time can block the individual dog from breeding. In these circumstances, I find it acceptable to raise, and sell, a ridgeless puppy. It must be remembered at all times that a ridgeless puppy does not suffer and, as a pet or in sports such as Agility, the dog can be great fun.

However, it is absolutely essential that the individual is not used for breeding. In a number of coutries, new ethical rules with the veterinary authority, or even national law, prevents the culling of ridgeless puppies, as the animals themselves are perfectly healthy. It is most essential that statistics are kept of ridgeless puppies in a litter. This information, used constructively, will eventually help us decrease the amount of ridgelessness.

Now, we come to a contentious issue. Assume that you are aware that a dog and a bitch, who are of top quality in temperament and conformation, are both heterozygote. Is it morally correct to mate this combination, knowing that there will be ridgeless puppies? My view is that where the parents might really offer advantages to future breeding programmes that cannot otherwise be obtained and, assuming you are totally open and honest and declare the status to puppy buyers, then this mating can be justified. There will, whether we like it or not, be random combinations producing ridgelessness, simply because we do not have enough information about the ridge gene status further back in all the pedigrees.

However, this is another of those cases when I must point out that I am talking of making exceptions, not of making the practice commonplace.

## DERMOID SINUS

This hereditary defect has been seen as synonymous with Ridgebacks. In fact, it can appear in other breeds of dog, and other animals, including man. The Dermoid Sinus is a skin development defect that creates a small external opening in the skin with a channel or 'tube' leading to the dorsal spinal ligament. The most common place for this to be seen is just outside the ridge area, in the neck, on the rump, or by the root of the tail.

However, take care! There can be more than one Dermoid Sinus in an individual animal, and DS can be found in other places, such as on the side of the neck, even on the skull, and on the flanks of a dog.

If the DS is complete, i.e. reaches to the dorsal spinal ligament, it is inevitably a problem that will lead to severe suffering, and eventually death, if not acted upon. The recommendation of most Ridgeback breeders is to cull a puppy with DS – I believe that this should remain the case, and

should not be prevented by legislation. In most developed countries, there have been successful operations to remove DS. However, in too many cases the full extent of the DS has not been removed, and the infections and sufferings, both for the dog and for the owners, have continued.

A Ridgeback that has had DS should never be bred from, even if the operation has been successful. There is debate about whether littermates of a dog with DS should be used for breeding, but as the true hereditary dependence and mechanism of DS is not known, one could, on a scientific basis, justify breeding with the brothers or sisters, with the proviso that buyers of any of their puppies would be notified of the situation. Personally, I find this argument questionable. Unlike ridgelessness, we are talking about a defect that causes pain and, eventually, death. Recently, an Australian scientific study suggested that increased intake of folic acid *before* the mating, might drastically decrease DS cases. Possible side-effects of folic acid are not known.

There are two remaining questions about this condition.

How do you find the Dermoid Sinus in a puppy, and how do you judge a dog in the show ring that has been operated on for DS?

When you have your first litter of Ridgebacks, it is essential that you get help from an experienced breeder to check the puppies. In theory, it is easy. You need patience lifting up the skin of the young puppy a little and feeling with the thumb and first finger, gently but firmly, for a 'string', that is the tube, connecting the skin and the spinal area of the puppy. You should test the puppy once he is 1-4 days plus, and for safety's sake, repeat the check a few days later. This search must cover all of the body.

With regard to a Ridgeback that has been operated on for DS being entered in a dog show, my position is crystal clear. The dog should be disqualified, as should a male which was not born entire, i.e he lacked one, or both, testicles, but has had the condition rectified by surgical operation.

**DERMOID CYST**
A less serious, though still potentially lethal defect is a Dermoid Cyst, where the tube ends before the dorsal spinal ligament. The condition, though

not always described entirely correctly as a 'cyst', as it should be referred to as a 'sack', i.e. a development without an opening in the skin, might, or might not, be inherited the same way as a DS. Operations are common, especially with true cysts.

**KINKED TAILS**

Kinked tails do appear in Ridgebacks. We are fortunate, compared to a number of other breeds, especially those who still have their tails docked in countries where it is acceptable, but we have to take the problem seriously. A kink in the tail is an incompletely developed joint, but is too often explained away with the excuse that "the mother stepped on his tail." The Finnish professor Sakari Paatsama was one of the first scientists to establish that a kinked tail is a type of skeletal problem. Viewed in this light, I urge each and every person breeding Ridgebacks to register kinks, and also to avoid using these individuals for breeding.

In the show ring I suggest a kinked tail should be judged as severely as a clearly asymmetric ridge, i.e. the individual should never get a CC, a CAC or a CACIB.

## HIP DYSPLASIA

Hip Dysplasia means asymmetrically or incompletely developed hips, luxation (i.e. the loose fitting of the hip) or arthritic developments, i.e. additional developments of bone structure in the hip.

The hereditary coefficient is mentioned between 0,2 and 0,4, that is, more than half of the cases are seen as related to growth, nutritional problems etc. This is one reason why, in my tips on nutrition, I advised against offering over-rich food and too fast a growth rate. One should, naturally, also avoid overdoing heavy physical exercise during the growing stage, especially with a rather large dog breed such as the Ridgeback.

In many breeds, Hip Dysplasia is the most common, partly hereditary cause of pain in a dog.

The best basic policies to follow in the fight against HD are:
• That all dogs should be X-rayed. Checking youngsters as young as six months of age gives a 90 per cent certainty of the results. The statistically ideal age for the X-ray remains two years.
• That all dogs used for breeding should have the results of their X-ray published, so that breeders always know the HD status of potential parents.
• Unless all four parents of the two dogs intended for a mating have satisfactory hip scores, even if the two potential parents are cleared of HD, there should be no more than one mating with the combination, until all their progeny are checked (at a minimum of one year of age).

Many countries and clubs have their own individual rules on Hip Dysplasia which must be followed.

My recommendations, for our basically sound breed, are based upon three things:
• Experience from Sweden, where research on HD has been carried out for longer, and more systematically, than anywhere else in the world.
• Comparisons with HD elimination programmes in other breeds, most of which have had more severe problems than the Ridgeback.
• The Swedish RR Club experience. The Swedish RR club was one of the pioneers, in the early 1980s, in demanding obligatory X-rays, plus the publishing of results. These results were for information purposes only, and there was no rigid ban

on breeding from any borderline HD cases. In 1975 Sweden had 35 per cent known HD cases among Ridgebacks. By 1983 the average was down to 5 per cent, and it has remained at, or even under, 5 per cent ever since.

The RR club principles have since been adopted as a common model for many other breed clubs. The beauty of this solution is that it is based upon knowledge – and an intelligent use of knowledge. Bans and mandatory rules must always be a last resort, to be used only in a crisis!

I need to stress that, if a country had a more serious and proven HD problem with Ridgebacks,

stronger measures need to be taken. In these cases one should remember that it is wisest not to introduce permanent bans and strict rules, but to set targets, i.e. a tough programme of control until there is, say, under 5 per cent of HD cases in the particular population.

Finally, on the subject of HD, I also suggest that elbows are almost as essential in a fast and mobile dog, such as a Ridgeback. I would suggest that when breeders have their Ridgebacks checked for HD, they should, at the same time, have an X-ray taken of the elbows.

## PARVOVIRUS

This is a highly contagious viral disease that leads to heavy diarrhoea and, in many cases, death, which struck the canine world in the late 1970s. Today no vaccinations give 100 per cent protection, so strict vaccination routines, combined with hygiene and common sense are required. Modern vaccines are found not to have any effects on reproduction, so you need to have no fear in vaccinating a bitch that is to be mated.

The recommendation is to give the first parvo injection to a puppy at eight weeks, repeating the vaccinations every month until the dog is six months old. You might also give one more injection at nine months, and then at the age of one year, repeating the vaccination annually.

If you import or export dogs, remember that the parvovirus, like so many other modern infections, varies and changes. So, if you buy an imported dog, he needs to be vaccinated immediately after arrival, with the local vaccine recommended by your vet. If you export a dog, make sure the new owner arranges for him to be vaccinated on arrival in the new country.

## RABIES

With the new 1994 rules for more open borders in Northern Europe, controlling rabies vaccination routines is a must. If you travel between European countries, excluding Sweden and Norway, you need a dog passport from your vet showing that your dog has been vaccinated against rabies within the last year. In some countries, dogs not travelling to other countries need a repeat vaccination every two years. My recommendation is an annual rabies shot in all cases.

If you plan to travel to Sweden or Norway, and you need the border clearance for the first time, official regulations must be completed seven months ahead of your first trip. You will need laboratory tests from approved labs (check with the authorities for an approved lab, and also an approved type of rabies vaccine) that the dog has attained a minimum level of antibodies.

You cannot enter the countries if your dog has been in a non-EU or non-EEA country for the last 12 months, e.g. Hungary, the Czech Republic, the USA, etc. The UK currently still maintains its border-protecting regime.

## CARING FOR THE VETERAN

A dog's life is short, and even the greatest and strongest, most lively individual will one day get those first grey hairs around his nose. However, the Ridgeback is a healthy breed and there are many, many examples of Ridgebacks being in great shape long after the ten-year barrier is passed.

There is a saying that "You cannot teach an old dog new tricks", which is completely false. You simply do not have the patience to teach an old dog new tricks, because old dogs have learnt plenty of tricks of their own to avoid being taught other people's tricks. The ageing dog can be one of the most treasured members of the household. He, or she, knows your every move, and every mood of the family, you can trust the dog completely and he or she is just great, great fun to have around.

One of the simple secrets of keeping an ageing Ridgeback happy is not to stop exercising him, either mentally or physically, when he reaches the veteran age. In most countries this is about seven or eight years of age as regards the show ring. Let the older dog feel you remember him, even if he can no longer enjoy the long, long walks or hours of play with the same agility.

Another important factor is not to overfeed the ageing dog. He no longer has the same amount of energy, and can thus eat less, or, preferably, the same quantity of food with a lower energy content.

If you have puppies, or young dogs, in your home, together with the old dog, do make sure that you allow the veteran enough peace and quiet, with the opportunity to rest by himself. In some cases, the old pack leader retains full authority over the young ones until the very end, but if necessary you should step in to ensure that he is treated with the respect his age deserves.

Good luck with your Rhodesian Ridgeback. May you have a happy, healthy and devoted companion for many, many years.

*Photo: P.O. Toerrisen.*